anythink

INSIDE OUTER SPACE

COMETS
and Meteors

Chana Stiefel

Rourke
Educational Media

rourkeeducationalmedia.com

Teaching Focus:

Endings- ed: Locate the words helped and crashed in the book. Write the words and underline the common root word. Then compare the endings. How does each ending change the meaning of the root word? Practice using the endings with another root word. What other words follow this pattern?

Before Reading:

Building Academic Vocabulary and Background Knowledge

Before reading a book, it is important to set the stage for your child or student by using pre-reading strategies. This will help them develop their vocabulary, increase their reading comprehension, and make connections across the curriculum.

1. Read the title and look at the cover. *Let's make predictions about what this book will be about.*
2. Take a picture walk by talking about the pictures/photographs in the book. Implant the vocabulary as you take the picture walk. Be sure to talk about the text features such as headings, Table of Contents, glossary, bolded words, captions, charts/diagrams, or Index.
3. Have students read the first page of text with you then have students read the remaining text.
4. Strategy Talk – use to assist students while reading.
   - Get your mouth ready
   - Look at the picture
   - Think…does it make sense
   - Think…does it look right
   - Think…does it sound right
   - Chunk it – by looking for a part you know
5. Read it again.
6. After reading the book complete the activities below.

Content Area Vocabulary
Use glossary words in a sentence.

atmosphere
comet
meteor
meteorite
meteoroid
orbit

After Reading:

Comprehension and Extension Activity

After reading the book, work on the following questions with your child or students in order to check their level of reading comprehension and content mastery.

1. *What are comets made of?* (Summarize)
2. *Explain what scientists may do if a giant meteoroid was heading for Earth.* (Summarize)
3. *What's the difference between meteoroids and meteorites?* (Summarize)
4. *How did comets help form our oceans and air?* (Asking questions)

Extension Activity

A crater forms from the impact of an object on the surface, such as a meteoroid hitting the Earth's surface. Let's investigate! Spread newspaper on the floor. Put about 3 inches (7.6 cm) of flour in a shallow box. On top of the flour add a layer of another color such as chocolate cake mix. Choose several small objects, like marbles or small rocks, of different sizes and weights to represent your meteorites. Drop each object from the same height of 3-5 feet (91.4-152.4 cm). What happens after you drop the object? How big is the crater that formed? What does the area around the crater look like?

Table of Contents

Look Up!

What has a head, two tails, and shoots across the sky? It's a **comet**! A comet's head is a giant chunk of ice, rock, and dust. Its two tails are trails of dust and gas.

Explore comets and other wonders as they zip through space.

The word comet comes from a Greek word meaning "long haired." Comets' tails flow like hair.

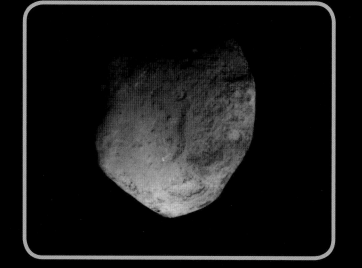

Comets look like dirty snowballs. They come from the far edges of the solar system. Most comets travel around the Sun. Their path is called an **orbit**. The Sun's light makes comets shine.

A comet heats up as it nears the Sun. Most of the nucleus, a comet's icy center, stays solid. Ice on the comet's surface turns to gas. A fuzzy coma forms. The coma is a cloud of dust and gas. It stretches out and forms long tails.

tails

coma

nucleus

head
(nucleus and coma together)

The Sun causes chunks of a comet to blow off. These pieces of rock and dust float in space. Sometimes they get close to Earth. The pieces burn up in the **atmosphere**, the blanket of air around Earth. They make streaks of light called meteors.

Meteors are also called falling stars. But they are not really stars. They are burning bits of space dust.

COMET VS. METEOR

	Comet	Meteor
What is it?	Ball of ice, gas, rock, and dust	Streak of light made by burning space dust
How often can you see it?	Rarely; once or twice every hundred years	Nightly much of the year; best in summer
How long does it last?	Many nights	A few seconds
Do I need a telescope to see it?	Almost always	No

Most nights, you may see a **meteor** or two streak across the sky. But sometimes the sky lights up with hundreds of flashing meteors. This is called a meteor shower. These light shows happen when Earth crosses the path of a comet's debris.

The Perseid Meteor Shower peaks each year from August 11–13. The Perseids are bits of the comet Swift-Tuttle. The pieces burn up as they near Earth.

The Sky Is Falling!

Many comets break apart when they near the Sun. Pieces of comets that continue to fly around space are called meteoroids.

Space debris that hits Earth is called a **meteorite.** Large meteorites are very rare. Most are bits of dust, pebbles, or small rocks.

In Antarctica, people can spot meteorites on snow-covered ground.

Scientists think that comets may have crashed into Earth billions of years ago, bringing water and gases to our planet.

The comets helped form our oceans and air. They carried some of the basic building blocks of life. Without comets, we might not be here.

Eye on the Sky

Another very big meteorite may have crashed into Earth 65 million years ago. The explosion would have shot a huge cloud of dust into the air and blocked the Sun's light. Many species on Earth died.

Could a large meteorite strike Earth today? Scientists use telescopes to keep an eye on flying space objects.

If a giant **meteoroid** was headed toward Earth today, scientists would take action. They might use rockets to nudge it off course. Or they might blow it up in space.

Scientists say large meteoroids may head toward Earth once every 10,000 years.

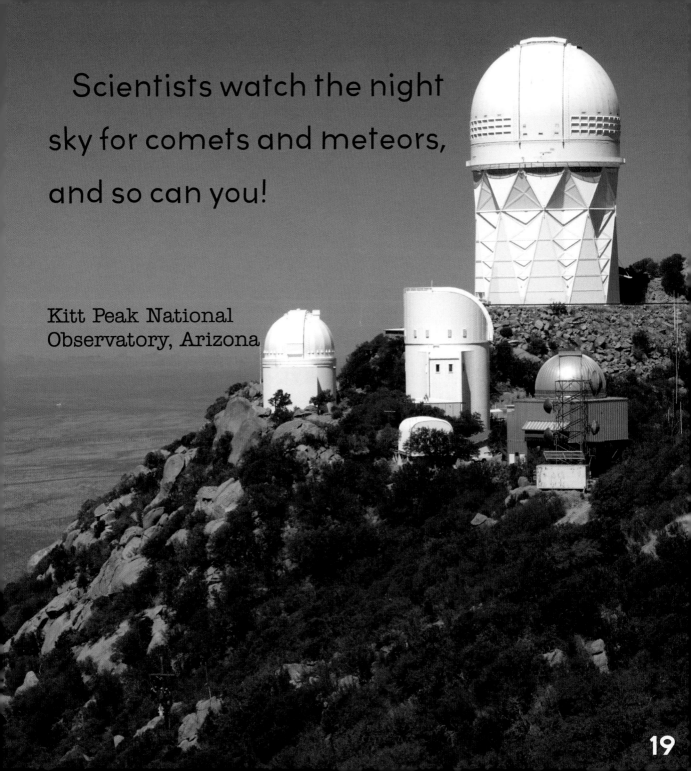

Scientists watch the night sky for comets and meteors, and so can you!

Kitt Peak National Observatory, Arizona

Comet Hall of Fame

ISON last seen in 2013, then it broke apart and disappeared.

Halley's Comet last seen in 1986. Next viewing in 2061.

Shoemaker-Levy last seen in 1994, then it crashed into Jupiter.

Hale-Bopp last seen in 1997. Its next viewing will be in the year 4380.

Photo Glossary

atmosphere (AT-muhs-feer): Earth's atmosphere is like a blanket of air around the planet.

comet (KOM-it): A comet is a chunk of ice, rock, and gas that travels around the Sun.

meteor (MEE-tee-ur): When a meteoroid or other space debris passes through Earth's atmosphere it creates a streak of light called a meteor.

meteorite (MEE-tee-uh-rite): After a meteoroid hits Earth it is called a meteorite.

meteoroid (MEE-tee-uh-roid): A meteoroid is a rocky piece of debris flying in space.

orbit (OR-bit): An orbit is a set path traveled around something else. A comet travels around the Sun in an orbit.

Index

Websites

http://www.kidsastronomy.com/comets.htm
http://library.thinkquest.org/3645/comets.html
http://www.neok12.com/Comets.htm

About the Author

Chana Stiefel has written more than 20 books for kids. She has a Master's degree in Science and Environmental Reporting from New York University. Chana loves to visit the Hayden Planetarium in New York City. You can see her work at www.chanastiefel.com.

Meet The Author!
www.meetREMauthors.cc

© 2015 Rourke Educational Media

www.rourkeeducationalmedia.com

PHOTO CREDITS: Cover and title page © Triff; page 4-5 © MarcelClemens; page 6 courtesy of NASA, page 7 © Igor Zh.; page 8-9 © Krasowit, page 9 inset © Navicore; page 10-11 © HARELUYA, page 11 inset © courtesy of NASA; page 13 © Nuttapong, inset NASA; page 14-15 © Nuttapong; page 16-17 © Catmando, inset NASA; page 18 © Digital Storm, page 19 © Bill Florence; page 20-21 courtesy of NASA; page 22 top to bottom © Pete Pahham, NASA, Navicore; Page 23 top to bottom © Nuttapong, Krasowit, Aphelleon

Edited by Jill Sherman

Cover design and Interior design: Nicola Stratford   nicolastratford.com

Library of Congress PCN Data

Comets and Meteors / Chana Stiefel
(Inside Outer Space)
ISBN 978-1-62717-732-0 (hard cover)
ISBN 978-1-62717-854-9 (soft cover)
ISBN 978-1-62717-966-9 (e-Book)
Library of Congress Control Number: 2014935658

Rourke Educational Media
Printed in the United States of America, North Mankato, Minnesota

Also Available as:
ROURKE'S
e-Books